T0195892

THE COVENANT
The Store is Closed

APOSTLE KENNETH HANDY

authorHOUSE®

AuthorHouse™
1663 Liberty Drive
Bloomington, IN 47403
www.authorhouse.com
Phone: 833-262-8899

Published by AuthorHouse 09/17/2021

ISBN: 978-1-6655-3869-5 (sc)
ISBN: 978-1-6655-3868-8 (hc)
ISBN: 978-1-6655-3878-7 (e)

Library of Congress Control Number: 2021919385

Print information available on the last page.

INTRODUCTION

I thank my Lord for the writing of this book; without Him, this would not have been possible. I also relied on the help of Atsuya McCoy.

I came to know the Lord in 1981, was called to preach the gospel in 1983, and was ordained an elder in the Church of God in Christ in 1986. I was anointed as a prophet of God in 2000. I was called to pastor a church, the Word of Life Deliverance Center, for seven years, and in 2015 I was called to be an apostle of the Lord. I now live with my wife, Barbara Williams Handy, whom I wed in March of 2018.

The word *covenant* primarily signifies a disposition of property by will or otherwise.

In its use in the sept, it is the rendering of a Hebrew word meaning "a covenant or agreement to cut or divide in allusion to a sacrificial custom in connection with covenant-making."

In Genesis 15:18, the Lord made a covenant with Abram. This is in contradiction to the English word *covenant*, which literally means "a coming together," signifying a mutual undertaking between two parties or more, each binding himself to full obligations. Let's look at this. There were two men, one a warrior and the other a farmer, who made a covenant between themselves. The farmer said, "When you are hungry, I will supply."

And the warrior said, "I will protect you at all costs, no matter what."

God has made a covenant with us, His people. He has said in Hebrews 13:5, "I will never leave thee nor forsake thee." In Psalm 91:10, He states, "There shall no evil befall thee, neither shall any plague come nigh thy dwellings."

After the flood, God made a covenant with humanity in Genesis 9:16. There are more covenants that the Lord made Genesis 17:13, Leviticus 24:18, Numbers 18:19, 1 Chronicles 16:17, Psalm 105:10, and Isiah 24:5: "The earth also is defiled under the inhabitants thereof; because they have transgressed the laws, changed the ordinance, and broken the everlasting covenant."

Isiah 54:10 and 55:3; Jeremiah 32:40 and 33:20; Ezekiel 16:60 and 37:26; and Hebrews 13:20: "Now the God of peace, that brought again from the dead our Lord Jesus, that great shepherd of the sheep through the blood of the everlasting covenant." The divine Genesis 17:2, Exodus 6:4, Numbers 25:2, Judges 2:1, Psalm 89:28, and Isiah 59:21.

Man with God in Exodus 24:7: "And He took the book of the covenant, and read in the audience of the people, and they said All that the Lord hath said will we do, and be obedient." Joshua 24:24; 2 Kings 11:17 and 20:3; 2 Chronicles 15:12 and 23:16; and Nehemiah 10:29.

Between men: Genesis 21:27; 1 Samuel 18:3; 2 Samuel 5:3; 1 Kings 5:12 and 20:39; and Jeremiah 34:8.

The new covenant, Jeremiah 31:31: "Behold the days come, saith the Lord, that I will make a new covenant with the house of Israel and Judah." Matthew 26:28 and Hebrews 8:10 and 12:24.

CHAPTER 1

Marriage Is a Contract or Covenant

1 Corinthians 7:1–16 (NKJV)

Principles of Marriage

Now concerning the things of which you wrote to me: It is good for a man not to touch a woman. Nevertheless, because of sexual immorality, let each man have his own wife, and let each woman have her own husband. Let the husband render to his wife the affection due her, and likewise also the wife to her husband. The wife does not have authority over her own body, but the husband does. And likewise the husband does not have authority over his own body, but the wife does. Do not deprive one another except with consent for a time, that you may give yourselves to fasting and prayer; and come together again so that Satan does not tempt you because of your lack of self-control. But I say this as a concession, not as a commandment. For I wish that all men were even as I myself. But each one has his own gift from God, one in this manner and another in that. But I say to the unmarried and to the widows: It is good for them if they remain even as I am; but if they cannot exercise self-control, let them marry. For it is better to marry than to burn with passion.

Keep Your Marriage Vows

Now to the married I command, yet not I but the Lord: A wife is not to depart from her husband. But even if she does depart, let her remain unmarried or be reconciled to her husband. And a husband is not to divorce his wife. But to the rest I, not the Lord, say: If any brother has a wife who does not believe, and she is willing to live with him, let him not divorce her. And a woman who has a husband who does not believe, if he is willing to live with her, let her not divorce him. For the unbelieving husband is sanctified by the wife, and the unbelieving wife is sanctified by the husband; otherwise your children would be unclean, but now they are holy. But if the unbeliever departs, let him depart; a brother or a sister is not under bondage in such cases. But God has called us to peace. For how do you know, O wife, whether you will save your husband? Or how do you know, O husband, whether you will save your wife?

What does God say about the convent of marriage in Ephesians 5:25? "Husbands, love your wives even as Christ also loved the church and gave himself for it." Genesis 2:24 states, "Therefore shall a man leave his father and his mother and shall cleave unto his wife, and they shall be one flesh."

How is marriage a sacred covenant? Marriage is a holy relationship between a man and a woman that was instituted by God. Even if a person is not married, he or she needs to understand God's plan and purpose for marriage, because marriage is about more than the couple saying, "I do." Marriage is God's idea.

How does God define marriage?

Christian marriage is a solemn and public covenant between a man and a woman in the presence of God. It is intended by God for their mutual joy, for the help and comfort given to one another in prosperity and adversity.

At the heart of God's design for marriage is companionship and intimacy; the biblical picture of marriage expands into something much broader, with the husband-and-wife relationship illustrating the relationship between Christ and the church.

CHAPTER 2

The Store Is Closed

Closed: not open, unwilling to accept, move so as to cover an opening

Store: a quantity or supply of something kept for use as needed; a place where things are kept for future use.

Quantity is defined as the number or amount of something.

All of us at one time or another have needed something and gone to the one store that we knew had what we were looking for, only to find that store closed.

I believe there is a spirit in the land that is coming against marriages; he works in our women to the point where they refuse to partake of our instrument. Women who know the Word of God know that it states in 1 Corinthians 7:5, "Defraud ye not one the other except it be with consent for a time, that ye may give yourselves to fasting and prayer and come together again, that Satan tempt you not for your incontinency."

The most romantic instrument is clearly the Wagner tuba; it's the most intimate and very quiet and can be extremely soft. It can be played anywhere and solo because it's a polyphonic instrument, and like the flute it's very often associated with intimacy.

Covenant Love

I do even when you don't; my promise doesn't depend on your actions. I will even when you won't.

Covenant Love versus Convenient Love	
Rational	Irrational
Thought based	Feeling based
Goal: Joy	Goal: Happiness
Goal: Pleasure of another	Goal: Self-pleasure
Sex as an expression of love	Sex as act of passion
Love as choice	Love as feeling
Unconditional	Conditional
Controversy processed	Controversy avoided
Divorce is not an option	Divorce is an option
Marriage is a living promise	Marriage is a piece of power
Love is what we do	Love is what we do until
You/us	Something better comes along
Forever	For me as long as it feels good; insecure

God's purpose for marriage is for a husband and wife to experience a love relationship in which they passionately pursue each other daily and in which the ups and downs draw them closer together to a place where true intimacy is.

CHAPTER 3

The Door Is Open

The door is open, a free or unrestricted means of admission or access. Whether you believe it or not, your mouth is an open door; the things you say can help you or harm you. Proverbs 18:21 lets us know that "death and life are in the power of the tongue, and they that love it shall eat the fruit there of." So ask yourself, What kind of fruit am I putting out there? Sometimes we say things that are not very fruitful, and then we wonder why something happening to us. Well think about what you said.

James 3:8 says, "But the tongue can no man tame, it is an unruly evil full of deadly persuasion or influencer of man." Salvation alone can help a man control it.

2 Corinthians 5:17–18 states, "Therefore if any man be in Christ, he is a new creature old things are passed away behold all things are become new. And all things are of God who have reconciled us to himself by Christ, and hath given to us the minister of reconciliation."

Reconciliation is the action of making one view of belief compatible with another. The circle of human life is continually excited by the tongue unless it is kept sanctified. Evil surmising, misrepresentations, falsehoods, calumnies, jealousies, envy, wrath, and malice all form part of the destroying flames from the tongue of the ungodly.

Fourteen Kinds of Tongues

Proverbs 18:21, NKJV: "Death and life are in the power of the tongue, and those who love it will eat its fruit."

James 3:1–11, NKJV: "My brethren, let not many of you become teachers, knowing that we shall receive a stricter judgment. For we all stumble in many things. If anyone does not stumble in word, he is a perfect man, able also to bridle the whole body. Indeed, we put bits in horses' mouths that they may obey us, and we turn their whole body. Look also at ships: although they are so large and are driven by fierce winds, they are turned by a very small rudder wherever the pilot desires. Even so the tongue is a little member and boasts great things. See how great a forest a little fire kindles! And the tongue is a fire, a world of iniquity. The tongue is so set among our members that it defiles the whole body, and sets on fire the course of nature; and it is set on fire by hell. For every kind of beast and bird, of reptile and creature of the sea, is tamed and has been tamed by mankind. But no man can tame the tongue. It is an unruly evil, full of deadly poison. With it we bless our God and Father, and with it we curse men, who have been made in the similitude of God. Out of the same mouth proceed blessing and cursing. My brethren, these things ought not to be so. Does a spring send forth fresh water and bitter from the same opening?"

Definitions

1. Surmising: to think or without certain or strong evidence conjecture guess

2. Falsehood: a false statement or lie

3. Misrepresentation: to represent incorrectly improperly or falsely

4. Calumny: a false, malicious statement designed to injure the reputation of someone or something.

5. Jealousy: jealous resentment against or rival a person enjoying success or advantage, or against another's success or advantage itself.

6. Envy: a feeling of discontent, or covetousness with regard to another's advantages, success, possessions, etc.

7. Wrath: strong, stern, or fierce anger, deeply resentful indignation.

8. Malice: desire to inflict injury, harm, or suffering on another, either because of a hostile impulse or out of deep-seated meanness, the malice and spite of a lifelong enemy.

CHAPTER 4

Death and Life

Proverbs 18:21: "Death and life are in the power of the tongue and they that love it shall eat the fruit there of."

Death and life are much determined by the power of the tongue, and the person who uses this power rightly shall live because of it.

1 Peter 3:10: "For he that will love life and see good days let him refrain his tongue from evil, and lips that they speak no guile: Let him eschew evil and do good let him seek peace and ensue it."

Five examples of death by the tongue:
1. The ten spies (Numbers 14:36–37)
2. Deog (1 Samuel 22:9–10)
3. Sennacherib (2 Kings 18:28–35 and 19:22–35
4. The Ammonites (Exodus 25:3–7)
5. Ananias and Sapphire (Acts 5:5–10)

Three examples of life by the tongue
1. Esther (Esther 7–8)
2. Paul (Acts 15:28–33)
3. Believers (Romans 10:9–10, 1 Peter 3:10)

CHAPTER 5

Rejection

1 Samuel: "For rebellion is as the sin of witchcraft, and stubbornness is as in guilty and idolatry. Because thou hast rejected the word of the Lord he hath also rejected thee from being king."

Rejection: the dismissing of a proposal, idea. "The union decided last night to recommend rejection of the offer."

1 Corinthians 7:5: "Defraud ye not one another, except it be with consent for a time, that you may give yourselves to fasting and prayer. And come together again that Satan tempt you not for your incontinency."

What does rejection do to a person? Being on the receiving end of a social snub can cause a cascade of emotional and cognitive consequences. Researchers have found social rejection increases anger, anxiety, depression, jealousy, and sadness.

What is rejection in a relationship?

In the field of mental health care, rejection most frequently arises in connection to the feelings of shame, sadness, or grief people feel when they are not accepted by others. A person might feel rejected after a significant other ends a relationship.

What is emotional rejection?

It is the feeling a person experiences when he or she is disappointed about not achieving something desired. It is commonly experienced in a quest of emotional relations, such as among romantic couples in social and group settings or in relation to advancement in the professional world.

CHAPTER 6

What Is Marriage to You?

Commands Concerning Marriage

The word *death* as applied to man in scripture means separation or a cutting off from God's purpose for which he was created. One can logically substitute the word *separation* for *death* in every scripture where it is used. It will clarify many passages to do so. Next, is your marriage falling apart? Are you eager for change in your marriage? Well, we want to encourage you that things can get better. If you are willing to change and work toward a better relationship, then that is the best first step.

- Grace Christian Church

CHAPTER 7

In 2004, I don't know what really happened or why she stopped talking to me. I would ask, but I got no response from her. And as time went on, I tried and tried, and so I said to her, "Let's pray."

But she said, "No, that's not my God; that's your God.

I said, "What?" I didn't know what to do or say after that. Here was a woman of God saying this; she was already saved when I got saved. This was the woman I had been married to for nineteen years and the mother of our son. Things got worse and worse; there was a thief in the camp, and he was winning. John 10:10 states "The thief cometh not, but to steal and to kill and destroy."

I don't remember the year. There was a time when I was asleep and my wife was not. A small demon ran and jumped in our bed between us, and she tried to wake me, but I would not wake up. She told me what had happened when I rose later on. The Holy Ghost revealed to me that was a spirit of separation, so I asked Him to let me see it. Up to this point, only my wife and son had seen it. The Holy Ghost opened my eyes so that I could see it, and when I saw it, I began to talk to this spirit and told it that it had to go. We began praying and fasting. I was reminded of Matthew 17:21: "Howbeit this kind goeth not out but by prayer and fasting." After we had done so, the spirit left.

As time went on, I tried to rebuild the family structure, but it takes two to make it work. I can remember as a boy, coming up in the late 1960s, how the family was a unit. Dad would work, and Mom would stay home and take care of the children. No matter how cold or hot the weather would be, he always managed to make it to work. In retrospect, I could see that my dad was a good provider. He took care of all our needs; he took on the responsibility that came with being the head of the family. Anything God puts you in charge of, you are held responsible for. Genesis 1:28 states, "God said unto them be fruitful and multiply, and replenish the earth, and subdue it; and have dominion over the fish of the sea and over the fowls of the air and over every living thing that moveth upon the earth." So as men, it is our responsibility to walk in our home as priests, loving and protecting our wives, just as Jesus is our protector, our provider, even our covering. We are to be like Him.

Philippians 2:5 states, "Let this mind be in you, which was also in Christ Jesus. It is our duty to love our wives even as Christ also loved the church."

Ephesians 5:22–27 states, "And gave himself for it; that he might sanctify and cleanse it with the washing of water by the word, that He might present it to himself a glorious church, not having spot or wrinkle, or any such things, but that it should be holy without blemish."

CHAPTER 8

Marriage

Hebrews 13:4: "Marriage is honorable in all and the bed is undefiled; but whore mongers and adulterers God will judge."

(1 Corinthians 6:9, James 4:4, Matthew 5:32)

Five Classes Not to Inherit God's Kingdom

1. Whoremonger: a male prostitute, a debauchee, libertine, debauchee, a person addicted to excessive indulgence in sensual pleasures; one given to debauchery. Libertine: a person who is morally or sexually unrestrained.

2. Unclean persons: homosexual, pervert: a person who practices sexual perversion; perversion any of various means of obtaining sexual gratification that is generally regarded as being abnormal.

3. Covetous men (Luke 12:15)

4. Deceivers (1 Timothy 3:13, Titus 1:10 and 3:3)

5. Children of disobedience (Ephesians 2:2, Colossians 3:6)

CHAPTER 9

Covenant

Let's take a look back at the word *covenant*. Here are some other words for covenant: compact, convention, stipulations, commitment, deal, dicker, transition.

Here is the definition of *covenant*:

> Noun; an agreement, usually formed between two or more persons to do or not do something specified. 2. Law an incidental clause in such an agreement. 3. Ecclesiastical, a solemn agreement between the members of a church to act together in harmony with the precepts of the gospel
>
> Verb; (used without object) to enter into a covenant. Verb (used without object) to promise by covenant pledge to stipulate.

Genesis 6:18 states, "But I will establish my covenant with you; and you shall go into the ark, you, your sons, your wife, and your sons wives with you." The term *covenant* refers to a formal, binding agreement between two parties a sort of treaty, pact, or contract. In Genesis 9:8–9, the verses are the formal conclusion of the covenant offering unconditional safety in the ark to Noah's family and many classes of animals.

In the style of a royal grant or unilateral agreement, this portion of the Noahic Covenant unconditionally promises that there will never again be a flood of the same destructive scale.

As shown in Genesis 9:12, accompanying the covenant was a visible sign of the agreement between God and the earth: God's rainbow. Genesis 17:4–8 section contains the fullest presentation of God's covenant with Abram. Eight different aspects of the covenant are presented in these verses; most of these promises are not new, but nowhere else are they put together in one place. The new aspect is where God changed the patriarch's name, thus indicating his authority over him. Instead of Abram ("exalted father"), his new name would be Abraham ("father of a multitude").

There was a perpetual covenant of peace after the flood, and God promised the waters would never again become a flood to destroy all flesh. The second explicit covenant in the Bible between God and a person (Genesis 9:9–17) is established with Abram, obliging God to provide the patriarch with descendants and a geographic inheritance for them that began in the south with the river of Egypt.

CHAPTER 10

A new covenant appears in Hebrews 8:7–13:

> For if that first covenant had been faultless, then no place would have sought for a second. Because finding fault with them, He says behold the days are coming, says the Lord, when I will make a new covenant with the house of Israel and with the house of Judah not according to the Covenant that I made with their fathers in the day when I took them by the hand to lead them out of the land of Egypt; because they did not continue in my covenant and I disregard them, says the Lord. For this is the covenant that I will make with the house of Israel after those days says the Lord I will put my Laws in their mouths, and write them on their hearts; and I will be their God and they shall be my people. None of them shall teach his neighbor, and none his brother, saying know the Lord, for he shall know me, from the least of them to the greatest of them. For I will be merciful to their

unrighteousness, and their sins and their lawless deeds I will remember no more. In that He a new covenant, He has made the first obsolete, now what is becoming obsolete and growing old is ready to vanish away.

Apostle Kenneth Handy

CHAPTER 11

Marriage, Christ, and the Church

In Ephesians 5:22–24, Paul addressed wives first, saying that it was imperative that wives were to be voluntarily submissive to their husbands. No external coercion should be involved, nor should submission imply that the wife is a lesser partner in the marital union. The submission is governed by the phrase as to the Lord. Christian wives, submission is a person yielding his or her own rights and losing him- or herself for another. Submission is patterned after Christ's example (Philippians 2:5–8) and reflects the essence of the gospel.

Submission distinguishes the lifestyle of all Christians. In Ephesians 5:25, Paul turned to the duties of husbands. The society in which Paul wrote recognized the duties of wives to husbands but not necessarily of husbands to wives. Paul exhorted husbands to love their wives, but Ephesians presents Christ's self-sacrificing love for the church as the pattern for the husband's love for his wife.

Husbands are to love their wives continually as Christ loves the church. The tense of the Creek word translated as love indicates a love that continues. Love is more than family affection or sexual passion;

rather, it is a deliberate attitude leading to action that concerns itself with another's well-being.

A husband should love his wife (1) as Christ loved the church (Ephesians 5:25–27); (2) as his own body (Ephesians 5:28–30); and (3) with love transcending to other human relationships (Ephesians 5:31–33).

Printed in the United States
by Baker & Taylor Publisher Services